Copyright 2008 by Stephanie Wincik

ISBN 13: 978-09725650-5-9
ISBN 10: 0-9725650-5-1

Printed in the United States of America

One Horse Press
23 Mechanic Street
Girard, PA 16417
www.onehorsepress.net

Cover photographs by Amanda Wincik

Gudgeonville photographs and audio by James McCann

We still do not know one thousandth of one percent of what nature has revealed to us—Albert Einstein

REACHING THROUGH THE VEIL: GHOST HUNTING IN ERIE COUNTY

BY

STEPHANIE WINCIK

It is through science that we prove, but through intuition that we discover—Jules Poincare

Part One:
Why Investigate The Paranormal?

More years ago than I care to count, my life was profoundly affected by a low budget, independent student film called *Billy Jack*. I particularly recall, almost verbatim, the content of a speech made by the main character while he was apparently channeling the spirit of an ancient holy man known as Wovoka. In that instant, I connected with an idea that I suddenly realized had always resonated with me as truth, but that my Protestant religious upbringing had never allowed me to really believe until that moment:

Heaven is not out there. The other world is here. Your people, my loved ones...there is a thin veil separating us from them.

Finally, an explanation that made sense. The thought of disembodied spirits floating around on clouds in some vague, unseen location in the sky never seemed logical to me. Not only that, but wouldn't it be boring? I don't know about you, but I don't find the thought of "eternal rest" after death especially appealing.

The idea that our spirits remain on earth, albeit on a different plane, seems an infinitely more interesting way to spend the afterlife. At least we could find ways to occupy ourselves, even if we need to haunt our loved ones for entertainment!

A thin veil. A curtain that some can see through easily and others cannot. But why? Why do some people, even while vigorously claiming not to believe in them, regularly see ghosts while others do not? That question alone seems intriguing enough to warrant further investigation.

In this book, we will explore the world of ghosts, spirits, and other phenomena through the eyes of those who seek to explain them— the paranormal investigators. We will discover their methods, motivations, and what they hope to accomplish. But before we get to that, though, let's take some time to look closer at the world of the paranormal and why there has been such an explosion of interest in this area over the past few years.

In 2002, when I was researching my first book, *Ghosts of Erie County*, most of the individuals I interviewed had a great deal of difficulty discussing their experiences out of fear of ridicule. Some said they had only disclosed these experiences to close family members, or perhaps to no one at all. Several of the folks agreed to tell me their stories only if I promised not print their real name, place of business, or any other identifying information.

This reaction is certainly understandable. Historically, those who claim to have had an encounter with the unknown, whether it be ghosts, UFO's, or any other being not thought to be of the "natural" world, have been met with accusations of insanity, involvement in witchcraft, or just plain weirdness. In reality, however, almost everyone I know has had at least some type of unexplainable experience. And happily, in the six or so years since my first book, I have discovered an exciting trend in the general acceptance of these phenomena. People today are significantly more open about their supernatural experiences. Evidence of this trend can be seen everywhere. On any given evening, you can surf your cable TV channels and find at least half a dozen programs focusing on ghost-hunting, UFO sightings, psychics, or simply "the unexplained."

In fact, I believe we are on the verge of a universal spiritual renaissance, when those experiences formerly thought to be supernatural will all be found to be part of our natural world. It appears that human beings, especially those in the western world who have been stubbornly resistant to accepting ideas we cannot yet prove scientifically, are finally ready to take a hard look at the possibility that there is an entire unseen world around us just waiting to be discovered.

Remember the voice-over at the beginning of the 1960s *Star Trek* television series? "Space—the final frontier..." Well, nearly forty years later, we are learning that outer space is undoubtedly not the final frontier. Exploring the invisible world that surrounds us right in our own living rooms is equally as exciting as the space "out there." A number of scientists, particularly those who specialize in the relatively new field of quantum physics, are leading the way for the rest of the scientific community in looking for concrete explanations of so-called supernatural events. They are seeking to prove what I believe most of us already know on some level—that the "other world" is just as real, or more so, as the one we can see and touch. Although I do not claim to possess significant psychic ability, and have never actually seen a ghost or UFO, the evidence that other planes of existence are as real as our own seems overwhelming to me. During the introduction of his popular television show, *"John Edward Cross Country,"* acclaimed medium John Edward says it best when explaining his ability to communicate with spirits from the other side…"How do I know?" he asks… "Because I do." So how do I know that in the not-too-distant future, the world beyond "the veil" will become real to us? Because I do.

In the next few chapters, we will take a look at some of the most common "supernatural" experiences reported by ordinary individuals—interactions with ghosts, orb encounters, and psychic communication—and find out how everyone, whether they choose to admit it or not, have already experienced at least one of these phenomena first-hand.

Ghosts

If you are reading this book, then you have probably already done some thinking about what ghosts actually are. The most common belief is that ghosts are the spirits of those who have died and are basically "hanging around" on the earthly plane, unable to move on because some powerful bond is keeping them here—family, friends, their home, unfinished business. Some may not even be aware that they have passed out of their body, such as in the case of a violent or unexpected death. Another theory suggests that ghosts are nothing more than residual energy left "hanging" in the air after the death of the physical body. This could be one explanation for reports of ghosts who appear to be repeating the same action over and over, such as walking up a staircase. These ghosts seem oblivious to the events or people around them. On the other hand, some ghosts reportedly have the ability to interact with the living and enjoy playing practical jokes such as moving or hiding needed objects, pulling off bedclothes, or opening and closing doors.

Contrary to what Hollywood would have us believe, rarely does a spirit exhibit malevolence or make an attempt to do serious harm to the living. Over several years of interviewing individuals who have a ghost story to tell, I have noticed the same types of benign activity seem to commonly occur in buildings where a haunting is suspected. Electrical appliances, especially lights and television sets, turn on and off by themselves. Pictures, books, and dishes fall off shelves when no one is near them. Doors open by themselves or refuse to stay closed. Objects left in one place disappear, only to reappear in another location. Cold breezes blow through rooms when there are no windows open or air conditioning on. Pets inexplicably begin to stare at corners of the room, often near the ceiling. Babies smile and coo at unseen persons. All of these occurrences seem to indicate the presence of a ghost, even though no one may have seen an actual apparition or physical manifestation in the area of the activity.

Not long ago, my daughter and I went along on one of the many wonderful ghosts tours available in Gettysburg, Pennsylvania. Our very knowledgeable guide told us at the beginning of the tour that we should not be disappointed if we did not "see" a ghost during the walk. He explained that, by some estimates, only about fifteen percent of encounters with ghosts come in the form of an apparition. Most interactions are manifested through hearing, smelling (yes, smelling) or feeling the spirit entity.

For example, as mentioned earlier, a ghost can be felt by the passing of a cold breeze or a cold spot in a certain area of the room. At a house museum near my home, two male guides conducting tours of the second floor both experienced what they described as a "blast of icy cold air that made my hair stand on end" when leading tour participants into the bedroom of the home's former owner. The owner had been of the Victorian era, by all accounts a lovely, genteel, but unmarried woman. Certainly one can imagine that a single woman of that time period might object to having strange men leading other strangers through her bedroom!

Some individuals have reported feeling "goose bumps" or a tingling sensation in their bodies when a ghost is nearby. Others report feeling that someone has actually touched them when no living person was close enough to do so. Sometimes one may just have a sudden feeling of uneasiness in the presence of a spirit. A number of years ago, my family and I took a vacation to Williamsburg, Virginia. While there, we had the opportunity to visit Carter's Grove, a spectacular former plantation house overlooking the James River. As always when walking through an old home, I was on the lookout for ghosts because oddly enough, despite a lifelong interest in the paranormal and a penchant for collecting ghost stories, I had never had what I considered to be a ghostly encounter until that day. The self-guided tour brochure described each room in detail and explained what the rooms had likely been used for decades before. The first floor walk-through was interesting but uneventful. When we reached the top of the stairs to begin touring the upper level, the first room we entered was a small but pleasant-looking bedroom decorated in yellow and white. The brochure indicated that the room had been occupied by one of the home's maids. On the surface, the little bedroom looked like any other simple sleeping quarters. The twin bed was made up neatly, and a spring breeze blowing through the open window billowed the white curtains out into the middle of the room. The moment I walked through the doorway, though, a feeling came over me that I can only describe as terror, and I had an overwhelming urge to run. Seconds later my daughter, who had been following me up the stairs, entered the room behind me and froze in her tracks. "We have to get out of here," she said. "Right now." The two of us literally ran into the adjacent bathroom. As soon as we were out of the yellow bedroom, the feeling dissipated and we finished the remainder of the tour without incident. To this day, I can think of no other reasonable explanation for our shared experience than that the spirit of the room's former occupant wanted her privacy!

Unusual smells are frequently a sign that a spirit may be close. Visitors to Civil War battlefields regularly report being able to smell the distinctive odor of a campfire in places where no one has camped for more than a century. A friend of mine whose mother passed away in a traffic accident experienced the smell of her mother's perfume filling her car as she drove down the section of road where her mother's accident had occurred. It is not uncommon for individuals to report smelling pipe or tobacco smoke periodically in areas formerly occupied by a tobacco user.

Another way that spirits communicate with us is through sound. Electronic Voice Phenomena, or EVP, has been found by paranormal investigators to provide what appears to be concrete evidence of the presence of entities we cannot see or hear with our physical senses. It works like this: during an investigation, a highly sensitive recording device is set up in the location of the suspected haunting. Usually several questions are asked of the spirit with adequate time allotted for a reply. All living persons present maintain absolute silence during the session, since even the rustling of clothing can disrupt the recording. Afterward, the recording is amplified, and often soft voices can be heard that were not audible to anyone present during the recording session. Sometimes it is impossible to distinguish actual words; the recording sounds similar to what one hears when listening to a conversation in another room—it is clear that people are talking, but not loudly enough to make out what is being said. Occasionally, though, EVP reveals spoken words that are distinct and unmistakable. More about EVP will be discussed later in this book.

EVP is not the only way that ghosts can communicate through sound. A common occurrence reported by those who have had ghostly encounters is hearing one's name called when no living person is nearby. Individuals can sometimes hear music coming from another room in a haunted location, and when investigated the room is found to be empty. An old Victorian hotel near my home houses a ballroom on the second floor. Employees regularly relate accounts of hearing music, clinking glasses, and conversations emanating from the supposedly empty ballroom, however when a living person enters the room the sounds abruptly cease. At this same hotel, a young waitress once insisted that the spirit of a woman named Rebecca was haunting the ballroom, and that the spirit would actually speak with her when she was alone in the room setting up the tables. Her story was discounted as vivid imagination by the hotel's owner, until one day when the owner entered the ballroom to inform the girl that she had a telephone call. As the owner came through the doorway, she distinctly heard the sound of a chair scraping along the wooden floor in the back of the empty room. "Did you hear that?" the startled owner asked her employee. "Of course," the girl answered. "That's Rebecca. She was just leaving."

Orbs

Probably nothing in recent years has stirred as much controversy in the world of paranormal investigating as the phenomenon of orbs. For those of you unfamiliar with the term, orbs are circular spheres of light that frequently appear in digital photographs. As one would expect, the initial reaction to these anomalies was to try to explain them away by attributing them to camera malfunction, flash reflection, water droplets, or dust particles. And certainly in some cases this is true—not every ball of light in a photograph is a true orb. However, even some of the earlier skeptics are now beginning to admit that the presence of orbs has become too widespread to summarily dismiss as dust or condensation.

In their groundbreaking book, *The Orb Project,* co-authors Miceal Ledwith and Klaus Heinemann reveal the results of their in-depth study of the orb mystery, suggesting that the glowing spheres are a form of energy that has always existed as part of a reality outside of our current human perception. Since the human eye can only perceive a narrow portion of the light spectrum, is it possible that this energy has always been with us, but was simply invisible to us until the advent of digital cameras?

As a participant in countless ghost walks and an observer of several paranormal investigations, I can attest that the presence of orbs has caused a great deal of excitement among those fascinated with the paranormal. However, as you will see later, the question of what orbs are and the approach to their study varies widely among paranormal investigators. Are they spirits with intelligence, or simply random balls of energy with no apparent purpose?

Generally speaking, I have found that most paranormal investigators tend to take a dubious view of orbs. Many still insist that they are nothing more than the dust stirred up by human activity. But even though I know that some of the investigators interviewed for this book will heartily disagree with me, I personally believe it is highly unlikely that orbs are simply dust particles with no purpose. In fact, I believe they are much more than that. Let me explain.

During my research for this book, I asked one of the investigators why he thinks so many people are resistant to believing in the existence of anything outside of our current realm of understanding. His very astute answer was that "people want to be logical." I agree. To most of us, it is logical to believe in what is scientifically proven, or that which you can see and experience for yourself, and to question anything beyond that. Certainly that view is understandable, but I also believe it is a view we have developed out of fear. We are happiest in our comfort zone, believing in what is familiar and safe. Dismissing something we do not understand as just being a part of our known world, like dust or camera malfunction, fits more easily into our current world view, and makes us feel more secure and at least somewhat more in control of the world around us.

Even though I have been a nurse for more than thirty years, I am still astounded by the amazing intricacies of the human body, more of which are being discovered every day. Surely whoever or whatever designed our bodies, not to mention the incredibly complicated machinations of nature, could also conceive of other worlds beyond our current capacity for understanding.

Have you ever seen a radiowave? I'll bet not, but microwave energy has always been there, even though we were oblivious to its existence until relatively recently. To me, it seems supremely logical to believe that there is more all around us than we can possibly grasp at this point, versus the limited notion that if we can't see or prove it scientifically yet, it doesn't exist.

With all due respect to scientists and those who strictly employ the scientific method when studying unfamiliar phenomena, I must point out that historically, science has often had to "catch up" with ideas that many people already instinctively knew to be true.

For example, you may recall the story of Dr. Ignaz Semmelweis. Dr. Semmelweis was a nineteenth century physician who observed that hospitalized patients suffered significantly fewer infections when the doctors washed their hands with an antiseptic solution before examining and treating them. He theorized that some unknown, invisible material was responsible for transmitting illness, and this material could be eliminated through hand washing.

As we now know, Dr. Semmelweis was absolutely correct. However, at the time, he was ridiculed by his peers, shunned by the medical community, and died soon after being committed to a mental institution. It was only years later that the existence of disease-causing bacteria was scientifically proven and therefore finally declared to be "real."

As I mentioned earlier, I believe we are on the threshold of a major shift in consciousness, and I think the orb phenomena could be one of the harbingers of that shift. People all over the world are reporting the presence of these glowing spheres of light in their photographs. Orbs appear in all shapes, sizes, numbers, and colors. They occur indoors, outdoors, and in all types of weather conditions. But are all of these images true orbs? Doubtful. In the afore-mentioned book, *The Orb Project*, physicist Dr. Klaus Heinemann describes the differences between the true orbs seen in photographs and those that are the result of "natural" conditions such as water or dust, and offers guidelines for determining the authenticity of your own orb photographs.

So... what is the final word on orbs? Only time will tell. In the meantime, look over the suggested reading section at the end of this book, do some reading about orbs and spirit photography, then grab your camera and do some experimenting for yourself.

Psychic Communication

Are you psychic? Of course you are. You probably just don't know it. Experts tell us that the average person utilizes only about ten percent of his or her brain capacity. If that is true, then what are we doing with the other ninety percent? Why is it even there? Of course none of us really know the answer to that question, at least not yet. However, common sense would seem to suggest that we all have the potential to do a lot more with our brains than we ever thought possible. Imagine your brain as operating very much like your home computer. Say you only use ten percent of your computer's capacity to send and receive your email, because that particular function is the only one you have been taught to use. Certainly that doesn't mean your computer cannot do anything else. It only means that its function is limited by you and your lack of knowledge about how to access and utilize its full power.

Why, then, is it so difficult for most people to believe that they, or anyone, could possess psychic ability? I believe it's simply a matter of conditioning. When we were children, we believed that anything was possible. The world of magic, fairies, dragons, and talking animals seemed as real to us as anything else. We quickly learned, though, by listening to our parents and other adults whom we assumed were wise and all-knowing, that any reality other than the one we experience with our five senses is only "make-believe." As we absorbed this "wisdom" from the well-meaning people around us, we began to deny the part of ourselves that we knew could do amazing things, and soon we just forgot how.

For some folks, though, their abilities were so strong from an early age that they refused to be placed on the back burner of the brain, so to speak. A very common theme among mediums and psychics with whom I have spoken is that when they were very young, they believed that everyone could communicate with spirits and predict future events. When they learned that wasn't necessarily true, many of them tried to hide their abilities in an attempt to appear more "normal" to others. Often, it was only after years of trying unsuccessfully to conceal their gift that they were able to finally accept themselves and offer their services to help others.

Most psychics and mediums insist that every human being possesses psychic ability. However, like any other talent, some people's psychic gifts appear to be much greater than others. For example, even though most of us are not math wizards, we all remember that one person in our high school algebra class who could always solve the problems faster than anyone else. And if you recall, that person always behaved like acing the test was the easiest thing in the world, while the rest of us struggled just to pass with a C. This concept holds true with psychic ability as well. Obviously, the majority of us have enough math skill to get by in our daily lives, but will probably never win the Nobel Prize for economics. Similarly, almost everyone has the ability to communicate psychically, but this talent remains dormant for most of us because we simply don't know how to develop it, or perhaps because we are not willing or able to put in the time and energy it would take to make it work for us.

Even so, I believe most of us can recall instances in our lives when our psychic abilities revealed themselves, if only briefly. The phone rings and you already know who it is. Or, during a conversation, you know what the other person is going to say before they actually speak the words out loud. You have a hunch about something you should or should not do and it turns out to be correct. Many of these instances go unnoticed or are attributed to coincidence, when in fact, it is actually you awakening the rarely-used portion of your brain that already knows how to communicate without words.

In the upcoming chapters, we will explore the world of ghosts, orbs, and psychic communication through the eyes of those who have devoted themselves to learning more— the paranormal investigators. Enter the realm of the unknown with James, Frank, Pat, and the others who work with them and share their passion. As you will see, their beliefs, philosophies, and methods may differ, but in the end they all have one thing in common—they are all truth-seekers attempting to reach through the veil and illuminate the other side.

There comes a time when the mind takes a higher plane of knowledge but can never prove how it got there—Albert Einstein

Part Two:
Pat Jones/Paranormal Study and Research

A couple of years ago, Pat Jones and two of his co-workers decided to take their passion for exploring the unexplained to the next level by forming the Paranormal Study and Research Group of Erie, Pennsylvania.

In the fall of 2007, Pat and his team conducted their first investigation into the long-reported supernatural activity at The Brewerie at Union Station.

A massive, magnificent-looking structure, Union Station is located at 14th and Peach Streets in Erie, and in addition to the Brewerie is also home to Erie's Amtrak station. Built in 1925, Union Station was originally intended to be five stories high, but the Great Depression stood in the way of that plan and the building remained at its current three stories. According to local historian and Amtrak stationmaster Steve Regruth, Union Station was once the largest train station in Erie. Before air travel was available to the general public, train travel was a hugely popular method of transportation in the United States, and dozens of trains carrying hundreds of passengers moved through the station each day.

Today, the interior of the Brewerie has retained much of the charm of the original station. Inside the strikingly beautiful rotunda, which is now the main dining area, remnants of the old station are everywhere. Benches from the waiting area are now the booths used for restaurant seating. All of the countertops are original, and one can almost picture the soda fountain that once stood in the corner now occupied by the bar. Old photographs line the walls, a reminder of the station's heyday when celebrities and politicians, including the likes of Babe Ruth and Harry Truman, routinely passed through its doors.

Not all the memories are happy ones, though. Reportedly, decades ago, a child named Clara was passing through the bustling station with her family. As the family moved into the area which is now the back stairwell, Clara stayed close behind her father as they climbed up the steps to the platform. Suddenly, as Clara's father turned around to say something to her, his heavy suitcase accidentally knocked her down the marble steps, killing the child instantly. Today, some evidence exists that Clara's spirit may remain in the building where she died. But more about that in a minute.

Chris Sirianni is the current owner of the Brewerie at Union Station. After years of restoration, the former train station now offers delicious food and locally crafted beers in an unusual atmosphere that somehow feels historic and modern at the same time. By his own admission, Chris was not a believer in the supernatural "until I spent a few nights in here." He is quick to point out, however, that he has never felt any negativity from the Brewerie's spirit population, and describes the paranormal activity as playful or comical rather than frightening.

Although the cavernous basement of Union Station, which contains dusty, antiquated tunnels along with a very old but fully stocked bomb shelter, would seem a more likely haven for spirits, Chris reports that most of the paranormal activity has occurred on the restaurant level and the second floor. Many of the strange occurrences in the restaurant are attributed to Clara. The stairwell where she died is located just off the kitchen, and according to Chris, staff working in that area are bothered by strange noises, lights turning off and on, and at times have heard their names being called out in a child's voice.

A particularly startling incident occurred just prior to the Brewerie's opening. A young

Stairwell near the Brewerie kitchen

man who was setting up the restaurant's computer system had brought his four-year-old daughter along one evening as he worked with Chris on the system. They were getting ready to finish for the night, and the young man called for his daughter, who had been running and playing across the room, and told her they were leaving. "Okay, hold on a minute, Daddy," the child called back. "I have to say goodbye to my friend. She fell down the stairs."

More recently, staff at the Brewerie have reported the sensation of "someone sticking their foot out to trip you" when walking down the second floor hallway. Chris himself has felt an icy breeze down his neck while walking in the same hallway, and a child's giggle has been heard by several individuals when no living child is nearby. In fact, so much activity has occurred in that area that Chris finally placed a chair and a globe in the hallway for the ghost to play with.

Psychics with no prior knowledge of the building's history have noted the second floor hallway as being a "hot spot" of spirit activity, however the spirits were felt to be friendly, welcoming ones intending no harm.

Steve Regruth agrees; he believes that whoever is haunting Union Station is a protective spirit. Steve has worked the night shift in the building for many years, and reports that he has never had a frightening experience. "It's more a feeling of someone looking out for me and overseeing the care of this build-ing...almost like a guardian angel."

When Pat and the rest of PSR investi-gated the activity at the Brewerie, some of their findings did tend to corroborate the sub-jective experiences of previous visitors and staff. Below is my interview with Pat where he discusses his background, his investigative me-thods, and the results of PSR's study of Union Station.

Stephanie: How long have you been studying the paranormal?
Pat: About fifteen years, informally. But I've only been doing it "officially" for about two years.

Stephanie: Did a particular experience spark your interest?
Pat: The main reason I got into it was because my house was haunted when I was a kid. I was sitting in the living room one night watching TV with my mom and my older brother. I remember this like it was yesterday; it really had an impact on me. A large white figure, sort of in the shape of a person came

right down the hall and into the living room. My mother and my brother both saw it, too. It didn't really walk; it didn't have legs or any motion of walking, it was just this figure from just about the waist up. It had a head, but it was faceless with no gender at all. It was glowing and you could see right through it. It came into the living room and stopped about six feet from us. My mom was sitting in a chair behind me, and I remember her reaching around me and pulling me close to her, and she started yelling at this thing to go away. It did, but it didn't just disappear, it actually left the room. After she yelled at it that night, it never came back again.

Even though we never saw that thing again, there were other things that happened in that house. For example, one night my friend Denny was sleeping over at my house. We were in my room, just the two of us and the dog. We were supposed to be sleeping but of course we weren't. I noticed that my dog was starting to shake like he was scared. That was weird because he was half pit bull and not afraid of anything. Then I heard footsteps coming into the room. I kept my eyes shut, and I heard the footsteps walk up to the bed and then turn around and go back out. Denny was sleeping on the floor, and he said he felt the footsteps beside him too. The next morning we asked my mom why she came into my room and she said she hadn't.

Another time, I woke up around two or three in the morning to hear pots and pans banging around in the kitchen. I got up to see what my mom was doing cooking in the middle of the night. It was dark as I came down the hall toward the kitchen, and I could still hear the banging. I switched on the light, and when I did, I saw a pot floating in mid-air. Then suddenly everything stopped. When I saw that, I screamed at the top of my lungs and my mom came running out of her bedroom, so I knew it wasn't her.

My mom still lives in that house. I've never done an investigation of the house, though. We did some research and found out that an old couple who lived there before had both died in the house, so at the time we just assumed it must be them causing the disturbances. Looking back on it, it may not have been them. Maybe someday I'll look into it some more.

Stephanie: What is your philosophy of the paranormal? Are there certain things you don't think could possibly exist?

Pat: I'm open to the idea that almost anything is possible. I want to believe...but I have a hard time believing until I see or experience it for myself. Like a UFO—I certainly believe that we are not alone in the universe, but the idea that they have ships and they come here to visit us, I have a harder time believing. On the other hand, when I have people telling me legitimate stories about things they have seen, then I have a hard time totally dismissing it.

As far as ghosts are concerned, that's something I never would have believed if I hadn't seen one for myself. I think there's two types of hauntings—one, where the spirit has intelligence and if you tell it to go away, it goes away. I also think there are residual hauntings—where the energy has somehow been retained and the ghost seems to be repeating the same activity over and over. For example, a friend of mine swears that a ghost in his house appears frequently in the middle of the night and goes through his bedroom wall. There used to be a walkway where his bedroom is now, so it's like the ghost doesn't realize that there's a wall there now.

Again, I want to believe, I guess because of that fear of death and the unknown. I believe in God, and Heaven, and life after death...but I think everyone has that little part of them that is scared to die. What happens next? Where do we go?

Stephanie: Does it ever bother you that people might think you're weird for doing what you do?

Pat: I know they do (laughing.) Even my family thought I was nuts at first. I guess maybe at least subliminally I was worried about that, which is why I took so long to actually form a group and say "this is what I do." It's a little different now because most people think it's cool, but we're still freaks to some people. I've been called a loser, I've had people ask me, "Don't you have anything better to do? Don't you have a family? Don't you have friends?" On the other hand, a lot of people also want to know if they can join us. It's a lot more accepted than it was, but a shocking number of people still think we're nuts.

Stephanie: So...don't you have anything better to do? Seriously, what do you like to do when you're not working or ghost hunting?

Pat: Spending time with my wife and my three-year-old son has got to be first on my list of things I love to do. Beyond that, I don't know where to start. I fly planes, I'm big into photography, motorcycles, I love to play pinball...I have an enormous curiosity. I can't let things exist without understanding how they work. For example, I studied chemistry for years so I could understand how fireworks work. I have a band...I actually built my own recording studio in my house. I play guitar, piano, bass, and sing...pretty much anything you can think of, I've tried it.

Stephanie: How did you learn how to conduct investigations?

Pat: My friends and I did a lot of informal stuff at first. We would just visit houses, take pictures, talk to people, try to figure things out. It wasn't until some of the TV shows on ghost hunting came out that we thought, for example, of using an infrared video camera. I didn't know some of that equipment existed. I credit those shows for a lot of our ideas.

Stephanie: How did you meet the others in your group?

Pat: We already knew each other from work, and we just got to talking about it one day. It turns out that we had all done a little research on our own, informally. Then Mark went to the White House (of the Battles Museum in Girard, PA) on a tour and got freaked out by what he felt in one of the second floor bedrooms there. So we set up an investigation there, and that was actually the first time we all worked together at the same location.

Stephanie: Describe the methods you use to do an investigation.

Pat: We always approach our investigations by not wanting to know anything about the place when we first go in. That way, we can all get our own impressions and compare them later, and we won't have any preconceived ideas about what could be there.

When we arrive at the location, we walk though all of the rooms separately, then we share our impressions with each other. I try to film everyone as they share their reactions; later I put everything on a DVD. Then we establish the areas of the house that we all agree need to be focused on and then we set up our equipment in those areas. Sometimes we measure the rooms and draw up a floor plan. We lay out where the windows are, where the roads are...so later if we see some unusual lights on the video, that helps us determine if it could be headlights from a car going by. We also measure so we can find out the rooms that are crooked. Often in old houses, one end of the room is actually narrower than the other, so if people say they feel a "closed in" sensation in that room, it probably is just because the room is actually smaller at one end.

Stephanie: How long does a typical investigation usually take?

Pat: We like to be there from about 7:00 in the evening until around 3:00am. A lot of people think activity is the highest between 8:00pm and 4:00am. I think that just might be because people are settling into their homes, its quieter, and people are just more in tune to what's going on than they would be during the day.

Stephanie: Can you tell me about some of your findings at the Brewerie?

Pat: First of all, it's interesting that we all picked the same "hot" spots when we first went through—we all picked the stairwell (even though we knew about that coming in,) we all picked the entrance to the beer garden, and we all picked the second floor hallway.

One thing we got that was very cool was an EVP. It was just me and Mark sitting at a table in the middle of the restaurant. We were the only ones in the room and it was locked. It was about 2:30 or 3:00 in the morning. In that room you can hear the echo when you're asking a question. We heard someone clearly say "help me" and there was no echo; it was like the voice was right next to the recorder. Mark and I didn't hear anything in the room at the time; it only occurred on the recorder. I played it for at least two dozen people (separately) and asked them what it said, and everyone said they heard the same thing.

We came back later and tried to reproduce it. We kicked everyone out of the room and sat at the same table. I said, "We were here before and you said help me...do you need help?" When I said that, you hear a little disturbance on the recorder. Then I said, "Come on and talk to us, Clara. Or is your name not Clara? What is your name?" After that, you hear somebody saying something, it's not a background noise, it's a voice but you just can't make out the words. I've played it for various people and they all say it sounds like somebody whispering something but you can't make out what it is.

I also had a very weird experience downstairs. It was in the area at the top of the stairs before you go down into the tunnels. I was in there setting up equipment, and the rest of the group was in other areas placing cameras. All of a sudden I felt like I was being watched from my right side. I swore that if I turned and looked, there would be someone there looking at me. I sort of ignored it because I was in the middle of setting the settings on the recorder, but after a while it got so overwhelming that I had to look. When I turned and looked, I saw what you would classify as a real orb. It was giving off its own light...this thing was glowing. It was about the size of one of those red playground balls, at least a foot across. It looked almost like if you filmed an eclipse; you could see like the solar flares being shot off in all directions. It was bright white, you could see through it but it fluctuated in density, and it gave off these wispy, cloud-like illuminations. It was just sitting there, and when I looked again it was still there, not like I just saw it out of the corner of my eye. I wasn't really scared, but I felt a tingling sensation through my whole body. It started traveling downward, sort of diagonally, and when it got to about eight feet in height (it had been about twelve feet up) it traveled pretty quickly, went around the corner and down the tunnel that leads to under the tracks. I flew out of my chair and ran towards the tunnel that it went down to see it at the other end, or if I could see it moving, but it was gone. But it definitely rounded the corner. That was pretty awesome.

Stephanie: What advice do you have for someone who wants to be a paranormal investigator?

Pat: We actually have a lot of people who ask if they can join our group. We've developed a three-page questionnaire that we give to people who say they want to be an investigator. We ask a lot of questions about their beliefs; we're looking for people who are a little skeptical and will ask questions and not just assume that everything they see is supernatural.

****

As with all three of the paranormal groups showcased in this book, to help the reader better understand these unique individuals and the reasons they do what they do, I have included PSR's mission, philosophy, and the biographies of its members as it appears on their website.

For more information about PSR, visit
www.paranormalsr.com

PSR's Mission is to:

-Help people in paranormal situations who lack the knowledge or means to help themselves.

-Debunk supposed hauntings by discovering and presenting proof of existing "normal" causes.

-Scientifically investigate paranormal phenomena without bias or prejudgment.

-Seek evidence in the support of hauntings or dispelling rumors.

-Document supernatural events as they happen.

-Educate people about mysterious occurrences.

-Assist the global community of paranormal investigators in developing a universal understanding of supernatural activity.

PSR Philosophy

First and foremost, we believe that we humans do not have any type of in-depth understanding of the supernatural. Various groups and individuals have wide-ranging hypotheses, but most of what we do in this field cannot be definitively proven or perhaps even conceived. It is akin to the Neanderthal attempting to imagine an automobile or a computer. Therefore, we make absolutely no claim to have any answers whatsoever. It is our intent to simply set up shop, observe for awhile, record some readings, go home, review the tapes, and report on our findings with an objective, unbiased mind. Most often, we come out with little more than a few chills and some creepy feelings. So we do not view it as a win or a loss, simply another experience.

Secondly, we enter each structure or place with great respect, both for the owners and for whatever might be lingering there. Just as hikers practice the "Leave No Trace" method, so do we. A lot of places we investigate are of historic value, so we do not mark up the walls or floors, nor do we move or remove any objects in the place. We are called in order to help people find some answers and to provide explanations, and we will do our best to do so in a polite, professional manner.

Finally, though scientifically unproven, we have a general belief in energy entities that coexist with us. There are so many ideas out *there that we cannot hold fast to their complexities; we simply believe there is something worth looking for and documenting.*

PSR members/biographies:

Pat Jones
Founder & Lead Investigator

Pat Jones has literally dozens of hobbies including music, fireworks composition, piloting aircraft, animatronics, pinball, electronics (gadgets, gadgets, and more gadgets!), commercial video editing... just to name a few! Combine these with strong leadership skills, charisma, and a deep fascination with the Paranormal and it's easy to conclude that the formation of this group was inevitable. Having had several first-hand paranormal experiences, Pat has an insatiable thirst for knowledge about the supernatural. It is this overwhelming desire to learn how things work and why that leads Pat to his ultimate challenge yet: understanding the Paranormal.

Mark Dunar
Investigator & Researcher

Mark Dunar acts as a PSR investigator and researcher. Having extensive knowledge of local area history as well as an ability to sense supernatural activity, Mark's input as an investigator is invaluable. Being one who is skeptical but also open to"other" explanations, Mark offers a troubleshooting mindset for both proving and disproving whatever we might experience. He is a good-hearted man who seems to draw people (and potentially entities) to him. Finally, from a business perspective, he is very good at acquiring contacts and establishing relationships with those who might wish to work with us.

Carrie Rodler
Investigator & Lead Evidence Reviewer

Carrie Rodler has many talents that are extremely helpful while enjoying one of her many interests: the Paranormal. Carrie has studied Qi Gong, which is a martial arts discipline involving the focusing of inner energies. She also has 15 years of reading countless books on the supernatural, the occult, and religions from *all over the world. Also, Carrie studies science and physics "for fun" and involves her friends in these fields when necessary. When not garden-ing, playing music or learning a foreign lan-guage, she can spend hours evenly focused on reviewing video evidence. Most importantly, she has the ability to explore an area with an open and unbiased mind, and she possesses the character and intelligence needed to accurately interpret collected data. She approaches each situation with a high degree of skepticism as any scientist should, but she does believe in the possibility of "other" explanations.*

Stacey Gross

Stacey Gross has had an interest in the paranormal since she was old enough to under-stand what it was. She has no verifiable firs-thand accounts, but hopes, through research and actively investigating alleged hauntings, to both understand paranormal phenomena more fully and to help those who are dealing with the phenomena to understand it. Aside from ghost hunting, Stacey enjoys riding and working on her motorcycle, writing fiction and screenplays, and listening to everything from The Clash to Beethoven. She has what could probably be described as an unhealthy bias toward classic horror films and, when there is time left over, enjoys reading anything by Chuck Palahniuk, Nathaniel Hawthorne or E.A. Poe.

There are more things in heaven and earth than can be dreamt of in your philosophy—William Shakespeare

Part Three:
Frank Grande/Erie County Paranormal

Frank Grande is the founder and lead investigator of a relatively new paranormal investigative
group known as Erie County Paranormal. Below
is what Frank has to say about what he does:

Stephanie: How long have you been
studying the paranormal?

Frank: I have been interested in the paranormal for many years after some experiences as a child and adult. I started studying
the paranormal more after Debbie (my wife)
and I had some experiences in our home.

Stephanie: Did a particular experience
spark your interest?

Frank: I did have an experience as a
child back in 1976. I was around six years old.
We were living in my grandmother's house in
Farrell, Pennsylvania. One night while in bed,
(my brothers and I shared a bedroom,) I woke
up and noticed a dark figure in the corner of
the room. It had no facial features, but you
could see the figure of a body. It started to
come towards me and I started to yell that
someone was in the room. My mother called

the Farrell police. When they arrived they came up the stairs, shined their flashlights, and the figure had vanished. No sooner did they leave, the shadow re-appeared and again it started to come towards me. My brothers could not see it. This experience is something I have never forgotten.

The next experience I had was in 1988. I was eighteen and was into using Ouija boards. Of course a lot of kids and teens made things up, and pretended to speak to spirits. That wasn't the case for me. I was living with my father here in Erie, and one night I decided to place five candles representing the five points of the pentagram around the board, not knowing that it was possible to open gateways or doors to the other side. No sooner did I light the candles and turned the lights out, it got very cold and the hair on my neck stood on end. I could feel something behind me. I do not know what it was, but it felt evil. I blew the candles out, turned the light on, and called St. John's Catholic Church on East 26th and Wallace. The Reverend told me to get rid of the board which I did, and I have not touched one in the over twenty years since that night.

The home my wife and reside in may have some activity. We have had our bedroom door open and slam shut, with no help from the wind. Once we were remodeling the kitchen; I was at work and Deb was peeling linoleum up off the floor when she felt a nudge on her back. She thought it was Sheba, one of our dogs, but when she turned there was nothing there. Both dogs were outside. So, these are some of the experiences we have had that have really pushed us into the paranormal field, and to help others with experiences.

Stephanie: Have you ever seen an apparition?

Frank: No we have never seen an apparition. That is the ultimate catch for any paranormal investigator.

Stephanie: What is your philosophy of the paranormal? What do you think ghosts really are?

Frank: The paranormal, I feel, and other groups would agree, is 80 percent fake and 20 percent real. There is activity out there, you just don't know when it will show itself. We feel that ghosts are spirits that have unfinished business, or do not know how to cross over to the other side, or do not even know they have passed away.

Stephanie: How did you learn how to do investigations?

Frank: Actually this is kind of funny. I was flipping through the channels on the television one night, and came across this show called *Ghosthunters*. We watched as these two guys from Rhode Island and their team went into a home with this high tech equipment, such as infrared cameras, digital voice recorders and camcorders. They went around asking questions, trying to get responses and tried to capture video of ghosts. We watched and learned from these guys. We understood what they were talking about when they said you have to look at everything scientifically, and do not go in expecting to find ghosts or paranormal activity.

Stephanie: What do your family and friends think of what you do?

Frank: My wife's side of the family thinks we are goofy. Some call us Mr. and Mrs. Spooky. Others think we are nuts. My wife's mother became a believer after hearing some of the EVPs we have. My mother thinks it is cool, but my two brothers think I am crazy. Our friends think it is cool, and support us 100 percent.

Stephanie: What do you expect to accomplish with your work?

Frank: We want to succeed in helping people understand that there is life after death. Spirits are out there among us, and with the evidence collected we can share our experiences, and help educate future investigators.

Stephanie: What do you think we will have learned about the paranormal in 100 years?

Frank: We will have learned better ways of communicating with and detecting spirits from the other side. Equipment will be more advanced, and possibly we will be able to one day contain these spirits and understand why they are here.

Stephanie: Describe the method or procedure you use to complete an investigation.

Frank: For starters, we meet the client/clients, and listen to their claims of activity. It could be the feeling of being watched, shadows seen on the wall or moving across the room, banging on the floor, voices being heard etc.

We then set up our equipment in the designated areas of possible activity. One person will sit with the client/clients so we know exactly where everyone is located, and we pair up, never go alone, just in case something does happen, this way you have a witness. Each pair goes to a certain area, asking questions on their DVR (digital voice recorder) trying to pick up EVPs (Electronic Voice Phenomena). These are disembodied sounds we cannot hear with our own ears. We also use an EMF (Electro-Magnetic Field) detector. Ghosts and spirits need energy to manifest, so by using this device we can see how much electrical energy is in the area. We start with a base reading, then from there, check for higher readings. If we get a high reading, we will first check to see if it could be the wiring or not. We had one case where the owner felt like she was being watched, but as it turned out her electrical box was not on the wall. All of the wiring was exposed, and the EMF detector went off the charts. So this can cause a person to feel they are being watched.

We also sit in the rooms to try and get a feel for that area, asking for the spirit or ghost to give a sign of their presence. We also check to see if maybe vehicles coming down the road can cause shadows to appear on the walls, or make it seem like they are crossing the room.

Cameras are also used for taking pictures. Always take two pictures of the same area; you never know if you might get something. We use infrared cameras with a multiplex DVR for recording movement in the dark. These cameras come in handy, being that all lights are out.

We use a digital thermometer for checking temperatures in the rooms. We start with a base reading. If the room is 72 degrees, that is our base reading. If the temperature drops, we try to locate the source. It could be a window or central air, but it could also be paranormal. Again, ghosts and spirits need the energy to manifest.

We normally run from 6-8 hours depending on the size of the home or business, and plus we do not want to keep the client/clients up all night. We then head home, get some sleep, review the evidence collected, which can take a whole day if not longer, depending on the amount collected. We then will go back to the client/clients and let them know what we have found, or what could be causing the claims they have told us. If anything has been found and we feel it is not anything harmful, we will explain that to them. If we feel there is a danger, then we would recommend to them to have a priest come in and bless the home.

Stephanie: Have you ever been scared during an investigation?

Frank: Not yet.

Stephanie: Can you tell me about some of your findings so far?

Frank: Our last investigation in June, we went to a home with claims of a shadow standing by a baby's bassinet, feelings of being watched, and the hall light going on and off. We did not catch anything on video, but we did catch a few EVPs. One, which sounds like a little girl's voice, said "help me." We got a male voice saying "I'll bug her at another time."

Down in the basement, my wife and I were talking about the wiring and how the EMFs were high but did not affect me, and after my voice on the digital recorder you can hear a man's voice say "help me."

Stephanie: What is your opinion of orbs? What do you think they are?

Frank: Some people feel they are spirits; we feel they are just balls of light. Orbs are just electrical energy not seen with the naked eye. We do not consider it a spirit, but they are amazing to see.

Stephanie: What qualities do you think someone should have to be a good paranormal investigator?

Frank: You have to be a believer, able to work well with others and be sensitive to the client's feelings.

Stephanie: What advice would you give to someone who wants to become an investigator?

Frank: If you get into the field, make sure you have an open mind. Expect the unexpected. Do not go into a place and expect to find paranormal activity right away, you may just end up disappointed. Do not be afraid.

For more information about Erie County Paranormal, visit their website at www.eriecountyparanormal.net

Erie County Paranormal

We are a non-profit organization formed to help people who feel their home or business etc., is haunted or has paranormal activity.

We are a small organization, which means, though we will have less investigators, there will be less clutter, and we will be able to get the equipment up and running faster.

Though we may be small, our efforts are not in the least. We put pride and effort into an investigation and full attention to a client. We attentively listen to every need and worry and abide by every guideline issued during a case. We are covering Pennsylvania, Eastern Ohio, and Western New York.

Erie County Paranormal Members/Biographies:

Frank Grande Founder/ Lead Investigator

I am 38 yrs. old. I am truck driver here locally in Erie, Pennsylvania. I have been interested in the paranormal for many years.

I had my first paranormal experience back when I was 6 or 7. I experienced a shadow person. It was no taller then I was and the only thing I could make out was the body. No facial features whatsoever. Something I have never forgotten. So now I am hoping to go out and help others who have had the same experience or other paranormal experiences.

Debbie Grande
Co-Founder/ Lead Investigator

I am 44 yrs old, a store clerk and housewife. My husband actually got me interested in the paranormal, even though I was a skeptic until my experience.

I had my first paranormal experience in the home I reside in now. While peeling the linoleum up off the floor I felt a nudge on my back. Thinking it was our dog Sheba I turned and there was nothing there. Both dogs were outside. They say when you remodel an old house, that you can stir up activity in the home. So I would like to share my experience with others who have had experiences themselves and hope to investigate to help others.

Justin Grande
Evidence reviewer

I am a sixteen year old high school student at General McLane high school. I however cannot go on an investigation until I am at least eighteen. I do, however, help with the reviewing of the evidence collected. It helps me learn what to expect and helps me to be ready for anything that should happen.

I am very interested in the paranormal, even though I have not had an experience as of yet, I am looking to help others with their experiences, and to help them understand the differences in paranormal activity.

Eddie McKelvey
Investigator

I am twenty-two years old. I am in the child care profession. I have never had a paranormal experience myself but I did find out that where I live, a young girl around the age of five had passed away back in the late 1800's or early 1900's. I am looking forward to helping people with their experiences and hope to put their fears about the paranormal at ease.

Tina McKelvey
Investigator

I am nineteen years old. I am working on going to college in the near future. I am second shift manager, and very interested in the paranormal. If children are involved, I feel I can communicate better and relate better. New to the group and has already made an impact with communicating with the other side with the Digital Voice Recorder.

Alyssa Grande
Evidence Reviewer

I am a sixteen year old student at Collegiate Academy; I have not been on any investigations as of yet due to my being only sixteen. I am learning the ropes as I help review the evidence collected. I am excited about it and cannot wait to help out in the field.

Not only is the universe stranger than we imagine, it is stranger than we can imagine—Arthur Eddington

Part Four:
James McCann and A.P.G/E.C.P.

James McCann, founder and lead investigator of A.P.G./E.C.P. (A Paranormal Group/Erie County Pennsylvania,) has been conducting an in-depth investigation of Gudgeonville Bridge for nearly four years.

Gudgeonville Bridge is an historic covered bridge located in western Erie County, Pennsylvania, just outside of Girard Borough. The bridge is one of only a handful of covered bridges left in Erie County, and almost since its construction in 1868 the structure has been associated with hauntings and unexplained events.

Having lived in Girard my entire life, I grew up hearing the multitude of legends and tall tales about the bridge and the surrounding area. Many of them, particularly those that have been told and re-told for over a hundred years, have no documented basis in fact.

One of the most popular stories concerns a farmer who had traveled from Meadville to Girard sometime around 1870 to purchase a mule. On the way back home, the farmer was leading his new mule across the bridge when a traveling circus floating on a barge down Elk Creek began to play their calli-ope just as they passed beneath the bridge. Reportedly, the sound frightened the mule (whose name was Gudgeon) and he refused to cross the bridge the rest of the way. This infuriated the farmer to the point where he grabbed a fallen tree limb and beat poor Gudgeon to death. After Gudgeon's untimely passing, the farmer returned to Girard and asked permission to bury the mule beneath the bridge. From that day forward, the bridge was known as Gudgeonville Bridge.

Since then, scores of individuals have reported hearing the faint sound of a mule braying while they crossed the bridge. Others have reported hearing phantom horses galloping over the wooden planks, and still others insist they have seen a ghostly horse slip past them in the darkness.

In the early 1960s, tragedy struck the Girard area when a young girl picnicking with her mother accidentally fell to her death off the steep cliff which flanks one side of the bridge, locally known as Devil's Backbone. After the child's death, residents and visitors to the Gudgeonville area began to relate accounts of hearing a child screaming and crying in the middle of the night.

More recently, a Girard woman, who by her own admission had no prior belief in the Gudgeonville hauntings, had a bizarre experience while crossing the bridge in her car. As she approached the bridge, a filmy apparition of a young woman holding an infant suddenly appeared in front of her, apparently intending to throw the infant into the creek. As soon as the woman got out of her car to investigate, the apparition vanished.

Because of the extremely high incidence of paranormal activity in Gudgeonville, the bridge is a popular location for both serious ghost hunters and not-so-serious curiosity-seekers. However, James McCann and A.P.G./E.C.P. are the first paranormal investigative team to undertake such a lengthy and exhaustive examination of what is really going on at Gudgeonville Bridge. At the end of this section is a series of photographs, some of them quite astonishing, taken by James during his study of the Bridge. The CD included in this book contains EVP recordings captured at Gudgeonville by James and his group. What follows is my interview with James:

Stephanie: What first brought about your interest in the paranormal?

James: When I was younger, about eight years old, I had an experience that I didn't really believe at the time. My uncle, who I was very close to, passed away. We were visiting his home, and about 12:30 in the evening I was upstairs when I felt something brush up against my leg. I got up and went downstairs, and when I did I could smell his tobacco all around me. That was the experience that really got me thinking. As I got older, I just felt drawn somehow to do this.

Stephanie: What do you think ghosts are? What is your philosophy of the paranormal?

James: I think ghosts are the spiritual energy of humans when we pass. At least that's what I want to believe on a personal level. On a professional level, though, I believe they are some form of energy, but we can't say for sure that they are actual human beings who have passed. I think that's the answer we all are looking for. Is it really us on the other side, in another dimension?

Stephanie: What do you think of other dimensions? Do you think there are parallel universes?

James: I don't know...I really have to experience something before I believe it.

Stephanie: How did you learn how to perform paranormal investigations?

James: I did a lot of research on my own, and I also joined an Erie group some time ago and learned quite a bit from them.

Stephanie: Do you find that different paranormal groups approach investigations in different ways?

James: I think there are some differences. For example, some groups like to set up a DVD system with a monitor and have several cameras linked together, while our group prefers to set up separate cameras. Overall, though, the procedure is pretty much the same.

Stephanie: What do your family and friends think of what you do? Do you worry sometimes that people think you're weird?

James: Most everyone is supportive of what I do; once in a while there's some joking about it. I don't worry much about what other people think; they don't know what I'm experiencing when I'm out there. People have come up to me at the bridge saying "there's nothing here." But that's just because they don't know. You have to be open-minded and some people aren't.

Stephanie: What do you expect to accomplish with your work?

James: Basically I want to prove the existence of the afterlife. Everybody wants answers, and I think the answers are out there. You have the skeptics of course, you have the debunkers, you have science. For example, the big thing going on right now is with orbs. Orbs are very controversial. Yes, ninety-eight percent of the time, orbs are dust. But, in my opinion, I don't think people should be out there saying they always are, because they don't know. Yes, I think true orbs are rare, but sometimes you do capture them. I think signs of a true orb are that they show illumination and they demonstrate some type of intelligence, like they are reacting to you.

Stephanie: Why do you think people are so anxious to believe that certain things (like orbs) don't exist?

James: People just want to be logical, I guess. But the experiences have to come from within. When you have the experiences, then you know it.

Stephanie: What do you think we will know about the paranormal a thousand years from now?

James: I don't know...I think we'll still have the believers and the disbelievers.

Stephanie: Describe the method you use to complete an investigation.

James: After someone contacts us to request an investigation, we usually start with a pre-investigation. We research the history of the house or the location and ask the person who called us to describe what's been going on. We make a list of interview questions and go through it with them to try to find out what they have been experiencing. If there is more than one person experiencing activity in the house, we interview each person separately. Then we go around the house and take EMF (electromagnetic field) readings. We locate any natural EMF sources like appliances or electrical outlets, and then we start to focus on the areas where most of the activity is being reported.

We take some temperature readings, and sometimes I run audio at the pre-investigation to see if I can capture some EVPs. Then I go home and review everything, and af-

ter that we decide if a full investigation is war-
ranted.

Stephanie: Have you ever had anyone
make up a story, or has everyone been pretty
up front with you?

James: Once in a while someone does
fabricate a story, yeah.

Stephanie: Does anyone ever expect
you to get rid of whatever is haunting their
house?

James: No, I've never really come across
anything like that, no evil spirits or anything. I
don't really believe in the evil side of things an-
yway. I try to focus on the positives.

Stephanie: Have you ever thought that
there might be an entity "trapped" in any of
the places you've investigated, like a spirit who
is unable to cross over? And what would you
do about it?

James: I'm not sure you can really get
rid of a ghost, although people with certain religious beliefs think it's possible through rituals
and so forth. Sometimes people want a priest
to come in and bless the house, so that's something they can do.

Stephanie: Tell me about what Natalie does.

James: Natalie (Smith-Blakeslee) is a psychic medium who goes along on our investigations. We don't tell her anything ahead of time about where we're going, and she comes up with some pretty interesting validations.

Stephanie: About how long does a typical investigation take?

James: Generally I like to go into a place more than once if I can. Usually the whole thing takes about eight hours.

Stephanie: Do you usually go at night?

James: Yes, we do like to go in at night. I think when there is less activity around, like when most people are sleeping, the spirits have more energy available to them. That's just my belief.

Stephanie: You've been investigating at Gudgeonville Bridge for the past three-and-a-half years. Can you tell me about some of your findings?

James: Probably the most compelling thing we've seen so far is three lights that appeared out there one night. Don and I were standing next to each other, shooting some video inside the bridge. All of a sudden these lights came out of nowhere. They weren't visible with the naked eye; they were only visible on the infrared camera. They were strange because they showed no reflection on the bridge, like you might see if it was someone shining a flashlight in there. When we looked at some of the frames from the video when it was slowed down, one of the lights appeared to be in the shape of a man. I can't say for sure that the lights were an apparition, but it is a possibility.

We've also had some amazing EVPs come across. I believe there is a woman out there because I'm always capturing her voice. I have an X-class EVP of her—the voice sounds like it is saying "Ruby" and when you reverse it, it sounds like "Believe in me." An X-class EVP means that it says something whether you play it backward or forward. I also have a Class A EVP from the bridge. Class A means that it is nice and clear, and everyone who hears it agrees that it's saying the same thing.

Stephanie: Have you ever experienced anything similar to what's been described in the legends? Like mules braying or horse's hooves?

James: Well, Don and I did have a weird experience one night when we were out there.

We were just getting ready to leave when Don heard a noise on the bridge. I had started to walk away; I was putting my camera in the car when Don called me to come back over. It was a strange, loud sound that we couldn't identify. Then the brush around the bridge started moving, like it does when an animal is running through it. The thing was, though, it was March and there were no leaves or foliage to hide anything. The sound circled us for a while, then it suddenly stopped as fast as it started. To this day, we still can't explain what that was.

Another time I was out there alone, and I suddenly had the feeling that I was being watched. After a few minutes, I felt like something was encircling me, getting closer and closer until it seemed like I was suffocating. I got out of there as fast as I could that night!

Stephanie: What do you think that could have been? Some type of entity that wanted you to leave?

James: Possibly. I have a theory that the three lights I captured on the video could be three spirits. I've always had an impression that there is a male spirit there who acts as sort of a guardian. Psychics who have been to the bridge say that there are several different entities there.

Stephanie: Would you say the Gudgeon-ville investigation is the most productive investigation you've conducted?

James: Yes, I have over 28,000 photographs from the bridge. Of course, not all of them contain anything paranormal, but some of them do. In a few you can actually see what looks like an apparition. However, when you look at photos you have to consider the matrixing effect—that's a phenomenon where the brain tends to see faces in things, sort of like when you imagine you can see animals and things in cloud formations. On the other hand, there are some photos where you can clearly make out facial features.

Stephanie: What qualities do you think someone needs to be a good paranormal investigator?

James: You need knowledge of what's going on in the field. You need to be logical...look for a logical explanation first. You need to be skeptical but also respectful.

Stephanie: What advice would you offer someone who wants to become a paranormal investigator?

James: Really look into it before you get into it. Feel out the field and make sure it's what you really want, because it's not always easy. There's a lot more to it than just running some video. But if you are really interested in the paranormal, then gain some knowledge, learn from those who have come before you, and just go for it.

For more information about A.P.G./E.C.P., visit www.myspace.com/apgecp

A.P.G./E.C.P. Mission/Philosophy:

We are a private, non-profit paranormal investigative team. We at A.P.G./E.C.P. feel we do not have all the answers, however our passion, drive, and knowledge can help in the understanding of investigating paranormal activity. We respect those who came before us and respect those who walk beside us.

A.P.G./E.C.P. Members:

James McCann
Founder

Originally a native of Edinboro, Pa, James now makes his home in Erie. Six years ago, after spending a number of years as a private investigator, James decided follow his passion and apply his expertise and experience to the study of the paranormal.

Don McDaniels
Co-Founder and Lead Investigator

Don met James McCann while both were studying the hauntings at Girard's Gudgeonville Bridge. Soon after, the two decided to create a formal investigative team, and A.P.G./E.C.P. was born.

Gary Askounes
Investigator

I have always been interested in the paranormal. But one day while walking my dog at a small local cemetery changed things for me. A light snow was falling and it was just my dog and I. Our foot prints went in, but there was another set when we walked back out. It looked like the foot prints of a lady's shoe. They started from nowhere, and ended nowhere. Maybe a total of five or six prints. Years later at a local covered bridge, I found the same foot print. Just one. That event started years of research into the paranormal. While trying to find some history on that bridge, I found James who also had an interest in that same bridge and had been investigating there for several years. We met up one night and he invited me to join APG/ECP.

Natalie Smith- Blakeslee
Psychic/Medium

The death of her beloved daughter, Carrie Ann Smith on October 2, 2005 from AML, an aggressive form of leukemia, brought Natalie

Smith-Blakeslee home to the purpose behind her extraordinary gift. Since early childhood, Natalie has communicated with spirit. After her near death experience in 1989 due to advanced anorexia and bulimia, the messages and communications became clearer and more defined. Today, Natalie communicates with those who have passed bringing hope, love and light to those they've left behind either one-on-one, in groups, via telephone, radio and television, or online. Natalie also hosts her own television show, Messages From the Light.

Dr. Steve Hodack
Investigator

I have studied life after death in all areas of the spiritual world. I am a Doctor of Metaphysics and also a Reverend. Metaphysics includes a wide range of controversial phenomena believed by many people to exist beyond the physical. I follow my Native American ancestral belief. I have explored the paranormal and have done investigations for thirty-seven years.

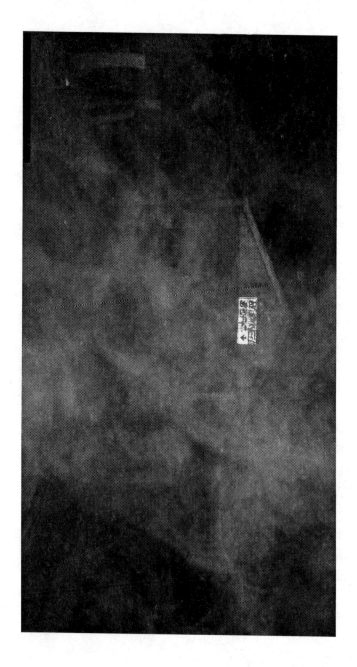

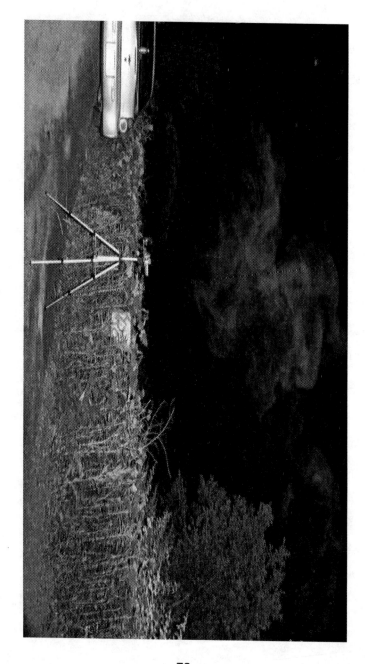

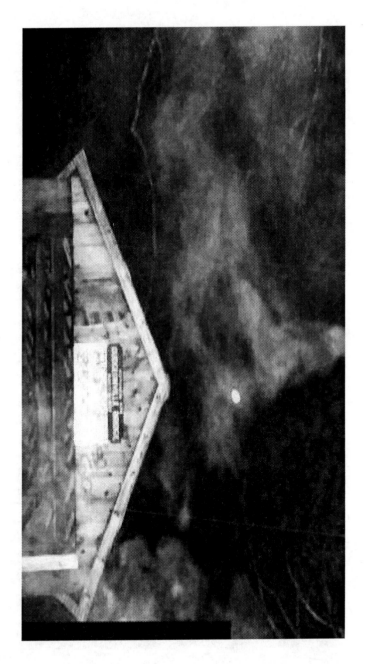

James McCann at Gudgeonville Bridge

About the CD

The audio CD included in this book was compiled by James McCann and contains EVP recordings captured at Gudgeonville Bridge. Some are difficult to hear and are open to various interpretations; headphones are recommended for best results. Below, James has listed, to the best of his ability, what he believes is being said on the recordings:

1. *Who's this*
2. *(unable to determine)*
3. *Only people take them*
4. *Derrick*
5. *I love to scare*
6. *Holy Spirit is coming*
7. *We're thinking*
8. *Listen to me*
9. *Went with the captain*
10. *Free us*
11. *We don't like them*
12. *Play and wait*
13. *Scared and lonely*

Acknowledgements

My sincere thanks to everyone who agreed to be interviewed for this book, particularly Pat Jones, James McCann, and Frank Grande. Your dedication and persistence in the meticulous and often tedious study of paranormal evidence is truly remarkable.

Special thanks also to Chris Sirianni and Steve Regruth for supplying the wonderful historical and anecdotal information about Union Station and the Brewerie.

Sources

Ledwith, Miceal & Heinemann, Klaus, *The Orb Project*, Atria Books, 2007

Christina, Frank & Teresa, *Billy Jack*, National Student Film Corporation, 1973

Edward, John, *John Edward Cross Country,* WE:Women's Entertainment LLC, 2008

Suggested Reading

Gott, J. Richard, *Time Travel in Einstein's Universe*, First Mariner Books, 2002

Kaku, Michio, *Parallel Worlds*, First Anchor Books, 2006

Emoto, Masaru, *The Hidden Messages in Water*, Beyond Words Publishing, 2004

Wolf, Fred Alan, *Parallel Universes*, Simon & Schuster, 1988

Lipton, Bruce, *The Biology of Belief,* Elite Books, 2005

Sweet, Leonore, *How to Photograph the Paranormal*, Hampton Roads Publishing Company, 2005

About the Author

Stephanie Wincik is a freelance writer residing in Pennsylvania. She has been collecting and publishing Erie County, Pennsylvania ghost stories and legends since 2001. Also a student of Civil War history and active in historic preservation, she is the author of five other books: *Ghosts of Erie County, More Ghosts of Erie County, Heroes in Disguise, Northern Lights,* and *The Journey: A Northern Lights Adventure.*